THE IRISH ELEMENT IN MEDIÆVAL CULTURE

BY

H. ZIMMER

TRANSLATED BY

JANE LORING EDMANDS

———

G. P. PUTNAM'S SONS

NEW YORK
27 West Twenty-third St.

LONDON
24 Bedford St., Strand

The Knickerbocker Press

1891

Electrotyped, Printed, and Bound by
The Knickerbocker Press, New York
G. P. Putnam's Sons

TO THE LATE LAMENTED

JOHN BOYLE O'REILLY

WHOSE KEEN INTEREST IN THE SUBJECT OF THIS
ESSAY LED TO ITS PUBLICATION IN
AN ENGLISH FORM BY THE
TRANSLATOR

PREFACE.

The importance of the work accomplished by the Irish monks in Central Europe during the Middle Ages has not been fully appreciated by English historians. It is not surprising, therefore, to find an almost total ignorance of the subject on the part of the general public.

The enthusiastic interest expressed by the late Mr. John Boyle O'Reilly, who himself offered to write an introductory chapter to the English translation of Zimmer's work, was the principal incentive to the translator in undertaking it. It is to be deeply regretted that Mr. O'Reilly's sudden death prevented him from carrying out his plan.

The essay originally appeared in the *Preussische Jahrbücher* for January, 1887, and *The Nation*, in referring to it, says:

"We should have called our readers' attention long ago to this remarkable paper which treats of the part played by the Irish element in mediæval culture. It deals with known facts of ecclesiastical history, and gives a most graphic picture of the successive groups of Irish missionary monks, their labors in France, Italy, Switzerland and Germany, their strength and their weaknesses.

"The author's style is clearness itself; his grouping and illumination of cardinal facts and features are masterly. We cannot attempt to condense what is already so concise.

"We can only express the wish that the paper may be translated into English.

"Nowhere else will the reader find such a trustworthy statement of what the Irish accomplished for the early Middle Ages."

I have inserted foot-notes compiled from a variety of sources wherever I thought they added to the interest of the subject or illustrated the statements of the author.

J. L. E.

THE IRISH ELEMENT IN MEDIÆVAL CULTURE.

recent work on the "History of Ireland from the Reformation up to the period of its union with England"[1] begins with these words:

"When a semi-barbarous or less cultured nation becomes subject to one more highly cultured, it generally receives as a compensation for the loss of its independence all the advantages and blessings naturally resulting from a higher degree of civilization. But a new condition of things was produced in Ireland through English rule; instead of arousing in the Irish mind a

[1] By Dr. Hassenkamp, Leipsic.

love and appreciation of English culture by the exercise of a moderate and conciliatory policy, calculated to lead up to a gradual and harmonious blending of the two races, victor and vanquished, the English managed, through a mistaken and blundering policy, as well as by intentional oppression and persecution, to bring about such a condition of affairs in Ireland that, in the first place, the social status of the Celtic race sank lower and lower, while, on the other hand, the tender germ of native culture was nipped in the bud, or failed of proper development from want of nourishment, and degenerated in quality."

These words explain the prevailing views of the present so-called cultivated circles of England ; they hold that at the time of the conquest of Ireland by England (1171), the former was, according to the ideas of the time, a half savage country in its relations to and compared with its conquerors in point of culture, and that its people obstinately set themselves in opposition to the blessings and advantages brought them by their more highly civilized rulers. Hence the hardest and cruellest measures which were laid upon Ireland and its people during the ages of English domination receive a sort of extenuation or justification. But the very fact that such views as these are entertained by England, weighs more heavily upon Ireland to-day than all her political and social ills; she rebels because England, not satisfied with stripping her of every present benefit, would even rob her of the consolation in her existing wretchedness, to be derived from looking back with pride over a glorious past. Ireland can indeed lay claim to a great past; she can not only boast of having been the birthplace and abode of high culture in the fifth and sixth centuries, at a time when the Roman Empire was being undermined by the alliances and inroads of German tribes, which threatened to sink the whole continent into barbarism, but also of having made strenuous efforts in the seventh and up to the tenth century to spread her learning among the German and Romance peoples, thus forming the actual foundation of our present continental civilization.

We live in a time when the civilization of the Occident, although drawing its origin from antiquity, and building itself up from its ruins, has established for itself a degree of independence destined to increase with every decade. However opinions may differ as to the degree of real progress reached by our present civilization, or as to its methods, or in regard to the question of the place which positive Christianity actually holds in it,—in respect to the past, all thinking minds will unanimously agree upon two points: that in those centuries of the Middle Ages mentioned above, it was Christianity that first carried civilization into tribes of barbarians (even according to Littré, who is one of the strongest adversaries of Christian philosophy of our age); and that it was the monks who, during that period, held firmly to the Church, and were its pioneers and defenders. Therefore we find that it was at the time when Christian civilization and ideas were commingled with the ancient, with deep respect for classical antiquity as a standard, that mediæval culture reached its highest perfection. Hence a greater or lesser knowledge of classical literature, particularly of the Grecian, was considered as a proof and measure of the culture of a single individual, as well as of the entire age.

In order to clearly understand and realize the significance of the Irish element in mediæval culture, and the part which the Irish can positively claim towards the civilization of German and Romance tribes, we must dwell a little upon the condition of the West before this period.

In the middle of the second century Christianity already formed an element in Roman civilization, and spread to the remotest provinces of the Empire, principally through their increased intercourse with each other, and especially by means of the campaigns of the Roman legions, even as far as the banks of the Rhine and into Britain, in spite of there being as yet no special missionaries to those countries. In the course of the third century it spread still farther, and in the beginning of the fourth it was decidedly flourishing in Gaul and on the Rhine and Danube, as well as in Britain, bishoprics being founded at Cologne, Trèves, and Mayence. In the second half of the fourth century Ausonius, the greatest Roman poet of the age, produced his enthusiastic description of the valley of the Moselle, while Arbogast the Younger, who had command of the garrison at Trèves during the incursions of various wandering tribes, was esteemed by Sidonius a model of the highest Roman culture in that region.

The German tribes from the Rhine and the Danube were now being gradually brought under the sway of Greek and Roman civilization through the medium of Christianity. But the internal dissolution of the Roman Empire and fresh incursions of savage tribes soon put a stop to all this. In the year 406, hordes of Vandals from the Upper Rhine invaded Gaul, ancient Germany, and Burgundy, and settled on the left bank of the Rhine, while the Huns under Attila made inroads upon these, and the Franks from the Lower Rhine burst into Gaul, making an end of Roman rule in that country. The Angles and Saxons had taken possession of Britain before this, and what remained of Roman civilization in Upper Italy under the Heruli and Ostrogoths was destroyed by the Langobards and their allies. The German barbarians thus ruined and blotted out the work of several centuries. So vanished in the sixth century the last remains of Roman culture which had lingered on at various points, particularly in Southern Gaul.

In spite of what Christianity had done for the Merovingian kingdom,

wretched indeed was its moral condition at the time of the death
of its famous historian, Gregory of
Tours, in 594. The disloyalty of
the Franks had become proverbial.
They had utterly repudiated Roman culture, appropriating only
its accompaning vices. Gregory
of Tours gives a true idea of the
state of ignorance in the kingdom of
the Franks, while he graphically
sketches the depraved condition of
the people and their ruler; he de-
plores the falling off of all striving
after knowledge, and he himself, de-
scended from a Roman family, having bishops among his ancestors, has
to confess that in writing in Latin,
he confounds the genders of certain
words, as well as the cases, and is
embarrassed by numerous other
grammatical difficulties. Merovingian records are written in such barbarous Latin, that when we find one

written in tolerably correct Latin, a suspicion of its genuineness is aroused, as it may be a forgery of a later date.

In Northern and Central Italy the standard of civilization at that time was not much higher. Gregory the Great, one of the most celebrated of the popes, who greatly strength- ened the foundation of the Roman hierarchy, knew nothing of Greek,— a most notable proof of the general low standard of cultivation in the West. Even two hundred years later, the learned and gifted Span- iard, Claudius, Bishop of Turin, when expected to defend his views respect- ing worship of images, of which he disapproved, before the council of Italian bishops, declared it to be a council of asses (*congregatio asino- rum*), and the Irish monk, Dungal, was called upon to undertake the defence of image-worship. These two learned adversaries, Claudius the Spaniard, and Dungal the Irishman, who met on the soil of Lombardy, are the representatives of those two countries,—the only ones which offered an asylum to Greco-Roman culture at the beginning of the seventh century, when it had declined in the West. Ireland was especially conspicuous in introducing it anew in the form of Christianity, principally into France, these efforts being made there when civilization was at its lowest ebb, and the country in its most degraded condition.[1]

[1] Dr. Reeves says of Ireland : " We must deplore the merciless rule of barbarism in this country, whence was swept away all domestic evidences of advanced learning, leaving scarcely anything at home but legendary lore, and which has compelled us to draw from foreign depositories the materials on which to rest the proof that Ireland of old was really entitled to that literary eminence which national feeling lays claim to. Our real knowledge of the crowds of Irish teachers and scribes who migrated to the Continent

Ireland never became a Roman province, and the hordes of wandering tribes that overran Britain and the mainland did not molest her. We learn from the " Agricola," of Tacitus, who gives us a minute account of the campaigns carried on by that great Roman general under Vespasian, Titus, and Domitian between the years 78 and 86, that, although those campaigns did not include Ireland, Agricola's curiosity was aroused by his proximity to it when encamped on the coast of Britain. Agricola wrote home to Rome a description of the country with what information he could obtain in regard to it, and stated it as his opinion, that Ireland could be conquered and held

and became founders of many monasteries abroad, is derived from foreign chronicles, and their testimony is borne out by the evidence of the numerous Irish MSS. and other relics of the eighth to the tenth century, occurring in libraries throughout Europe."

by one legion, being considerably
smaller than Britain, and declared it
would be a profitable acquisition for
Rome as held against the Britons.[1]
But the fact of Ireland never coming
under the dominion of Rome greatly
accounts for the Irish tribes and the
Pictish and Caledonian mountaineers
being the only portions of the Celtic
race which retained their independence and social characteristics.
These unsubdued Celtic tribes were
reserved for a great purpose,—to in-
augurate the evangelization of Central
Europe. Following the nomadic instincts of their race, they were destined to be pioneers in the missionary
history of Europe, during the decay
of the Roman Empire, and while the
Teutonic tribes were as yet in a state
of semi-barbarism.

Alive as the Irish race was to

[1] From Agricola we have the earliest notice of
Ireland in real history.

religious impressions, Christianity, which was preached among them by British missionaries in the third and fourth centuries, found in them receptive and appreciative pupils. In 430 Pope Celestine sent Palladius[1] as a Roman bishop to the converted Scots, according to Bede's testimony [*cujus (sc. Theodosii) anno imperii octavo Palladius ad Scottos in Christum credentes a pontifice Romanæ ecclesiæ Celestino primus mittitur episcopus. Beda., Hist. gentis Angl., i., 13*]. The *Scots* mentioned in the Middle Ages are synonymous with the Celtic population of Ireland, and were not to be distinguished from that people that early wandered through the northern part of Britain and settled in the Highlands.[2]

[1] "Palladius was consecrated by the pope and sent to those Scots (or Irish) believing in Christ as their first bishop."

[2] "Whenever, in the first three centuries, the term *Scot* occurs it always means *Irishman.*

While on the mainland and in Britain budding Christianity and the germs of Western culture, such as it was, were effectually trodden under foot by the various hordes of Van-

During the first seven centuries the Picts were the inhabitants of modern Scotland. It was not until the eleventh or twelfth century that the term Scotland or Scotia was applied in its modern sense."—Rev. G. T. Stokes' " Ireland and the Celtic Church."

The author of " Early Christian Art in Ireland " thus quotes from Reeves' " Adamnan " :

" The early Christian ·art of Ireland may well be termed Scotic as well as Irish, just as the first missionaries from Ireland to the Continent were termed Scots, Ireland having borne the name of Scotia for many centuries before it was transferred to North Britain, and foreign chroniclers of the ninth century speak of ' Hibernia, island of the Scots,' when referring to events in Ireland regarding which corresponding entries are found in the annals of that country."

Again this author says : " From Ireland the practice of the art of illumination spread side by side with religion to Iona, thence to Melrose and Lindisfarne ; and, distinct as its character is from the art of the Teutonic nations, it was

dals, Alemanni, Huns, Franks, Heruli, Langobards, Angles, and Saxons, and the Merovingian kingdom sank lower and lower,—when universal crudeness and depravity seemed to

henceforward misnamed Anglo-Saxon in England, while on the Continent it was termed Anglo-Saxon or Scottish. The fact that Anglo-Saxon MSS. exist in England with Irish decoration led to the misnomer Anglo-Saxon for this style until Waagen, who had sufficient knowledge of both schools of illumination, drew the dividing line between them. The mistake, however, led to much confusion in the Continental libraries, where even manuscripts written as well as illuminated by Irish scribes, were frequently named Anglo-Saxon. It is only of late that writers on the subject have learned that North Britain was not termed Scotland till the close of the ninth century, whereas the island of Ireland had for so many centuries borne the name of Scotia. The confusion of this Scotic or Irish art with Anglo-Saxon naturally arose on the Continent from the fact that MSS. written in Anglo-Saxon were often illuminated either by Irish artists or by monks who had learned their art in Ireland.

" Art in general of this period attained a more

have gained the upper hand, and the entire West threatened to sink hopelessly into barbarism, the Irish established several seminaries of learning in their own country. Bangor and

beautiful result in Ireland than elsewhere, because in the hands of a people possessed of a fine artistic instinct. But as regards the drawing of the human face and figure in the pictures contained in the otherwise beautiful books of the Irish scribes, nothing more hideous or barbarous can be well conceived. It seems impossible that they could have been drawn from nature, but rather seem reminiscences of some rude Byzantine prototype. Thence we conclude that in the Carlovingian MSS. of the ninth century we see not only a mixture of styles, but that, in the introduction of Irish decoration, we have examples of the engrafting of an archaic style upon another of later date ; a style that had died out of Italy and Southern Gaul, but lived on in Ireland to return there centuries later. In Ireland its character had been modified by absorbing whatever designs prevailed in the country at the time of the introduction of Christianity, and thus modified, it was spread throughout Europe again by the Irish scribes, though it never prevailed outside their sphere, and finally died out with them.

Armagh in Ulster, Clonmacnois, near
the boundaries of Leinster and Con-
naught, and Lismore in the South
were, at the end of the sixth century,
the most prominent and flourishing

To the designer of the present day, who strives
to adopt the ancient Irish forms to present uses,
nothing could be more helpful than the study of
those Carlovingian MSS., which are remarkably
beautiful.

" Interlaced patterns and knot-work, strongly
resembling Irish designs, are commonly met with
at Ravenna, in the older churches of Lombardy,
and at Sant' Abbondio, at Como, and not unfre-
quently appear in Byzantine MSS., while in the
carvings on the Syrian churches of the second
and third centuries, as well as the early churches
at Georgia, such interlaced ornament is constantly used.

" The manuscripts which remain in Italy as
evidence of the labors oi the Irish monks in
that country, are to be seen in the Ambrosian
Library in Milan, in the University Library of
Turin, and in the Real Biblioteca Borbonica,
Naples. All these manuscripts are said to have
been brought originally from Bobio, a monastery
in Piedmont, founded by Columbanus in the
year 613."

monasteries in Ireland. The standard of learning was much higher than
with Gregory the Great and his followers. It was derived without inter-
ruption from the learning of the
fourth century, from men such as
Ambrose, Jerome, and Augustine.
Here also were to be found such
specimens of classical literature as
Virgil's works among the ecclesiastical writings, and an acquaintance
with Greek authors as well, beside
the opportunity of free access to the
very first sources of Christianity.

At the beginning of the sixth
century these Irish Christians were
seized with an unconquerable impulse to wander afar and preach
Christianity to the heathen. In 563
Columba, with twelve confederates,
left Ireland and founded a monastery
on a small island off the coast of
Scotland (Iona or Hy), through the
influence of which the Scots and

Picts of Britain became converted to Christianity, twenty-three missions among the Scots and eighteen in the country of the Picts having been established at the death of Columba (597).[1]   Under his third successor the heathen Saxons were converted ; Aedan, summoned by Osward of Northumbria, having labored among them from 635 to 651 as missionary, abbot, and bishop.   His successors, Finnan and Colman, worthily carried on his work, and introduced Christianity into other Anglo-Saxon

[1] Columba and Columbanus, both born in the sixth century, have been confounded even by eminent scholars.   Columba was born in Ulster, and Columbanus in Leinster.   The one in 521, the other in 543.   Columba was the apostle of Scotland or Caledonia.   Columbanus never set foot in Scotland.   He was the apostle of Burgundy, Switzerland, and Italy.   Columba spent his life among the Pictish pagans of North Britain ; Columbanus labored among the pagans of Central Europe.—Stokes' " Ireland and the Celtic Church," p. 132.

kingdoms near East Anglia, Mercia, and Essex.

One of the most celebrated monasteries of Ireland was founded at Bangor in Ulster at the end of the sixth century. From this monastery at the time (590) that Gregory of Tours, the historian of the Franks, brought out his denunciation of the corruption of his people, an Irishman, a native of Leinster, bearing the ecclesiastical and Latin name of Columbanus, set forth with twelve companions and assistants to preach the gospel to the heathen. He landed in France, and finding Christianity in a sinking condition, decided to settle in the Vosges mountains and establish a mission there (Anagratum). The number of converts increased so fast that he was soon obliged to found another upon the ruins of a forsaken Roman bath establishment at Luxovium (Luxeuil), which be-

came in course of time a most fruitful centre of ecclesiastical and monastic life.   In these two places, as well
as at Fontaines, a mission station
founded somewhat later on, Columbanus and his companions worked
successfully for more than ten years.
But the intrepidity with which he
approached and dealt with these
degenerate Merovingians drew upon
him the hatred of the Queen Regent
Brunhilde. Ecclesiastical differences
arose with the Gallic clergy ; he was
driven with his companions from this
field of their active labors and obliged
to flee to Ireland. Being detained by
contrary winds in the mouth of the
Loire, he interpreted this as a sign
from on high that it was his duty to
remain. So, in 610, he wandered
into the country of the Alemanni,
where he labored as a missionary
under the patronage of Theudebert,
in Bregenz, on Lake Constance.

Thence, in 613, he went to seek the patronage of the Langobard princess, Theudelinde, and founded the Bobio monastery at the foot of the Apennines, between Genoa and Milan, which throughout the Middle Ages bore a high reputation as a seat of learning and culture in the very broadest sense. He died there in 615.[1]

[1] Columbanus was, in many respects, the greatest, bravest, most thoroughly national, and most representative of all the warriors of the cross sent forth from Irish shores. Born in Leinster, A.D. 543, he was educated first of all on one of the islands of Lough Erne. Thence he migrated to Bangor, which was then at the height of its fame as a place where the greatest attainments in learning and sanctity were possible. We are apt to undervalue the studies of these ancient monasteries, just as we, in our intellectual conceit, are apt to undervalue all mediæval learning, because the men of those times knew nothing of the daily press, photography, electricity, or gunpowder. In monasteries like Bangor, the range of studies was a wide one, and it must have been a thoroughly equipped and vigorous seat of learning in the

The Irish monk Gallus (St. Gall) with others had joined Columbanus on his mission among the heathen, sharing with him his trials and difficulties like a faithful comrade, but at the time of Columbanus' depart-

latter half of the sixth century, when it could have despatched such a trained and even elegant scholar as Columbanus to convert the pagans of France. The proofs of his learning are evident to any student of his writings. The scholarship of them is manifest. He wrote good Latin verses, full of quaint, metrical conceits, both in the classical and monkish rhyming style. Allusions to pagan and Christian antiquity abound in his poems. Where did he acquire this scholarship? His life on the Continent was one of rough, vigorous, all-absorbing, practical effort, leaving no time for such studies. Even did time or leisure permit, the opportunity was wanting, for the Continent was at that time plunged in utter darkness, literary as well as spiritual. St. Columbanus, we therefore conclude, gained his extensive knowledge and eloquent scholarship at the abbeys of Bangor and Lough Erne.

France was, toward the end of the sixth century, a bye-word throughout Europe for immorality and irreligion. When we think of the

ure for Lombardy, was forced by
illness to remain behind with the
Alemanni, one of whom hospitably
cared for him until his health was
restored. Gallus then collected together twelve associates and set out

Gaul of that period, we must not think of it as
it was in the fourth and fifth centuries, the age
of Hilary of Poitiers, of a Martin of Tours, or a
Germanus of Auxerre. For a hundred years
back, it had been the prey of every invader.
Milman, in his "Latin Christianity," says: "It
is difficult to conceive a more dark and odious
state of society than that of France under her
Merovingian kings, the descendants of Clovis,
as described by Gregory of Tours. In the con-
flict of coalition of barbarism with Roman
Christianity, barbarism has introdüced into
Christianity all its ferocity, with none of its
generosity or magnanimity. Its energy shows
itself in atrocity of cruelty, and even of sensual-
ity. Throughout, assassinations, parricides, and
fratricides intermingle with adulteries and rapes.
That King Clotaire should burn alive his rebel-
lious son with his wife and daughter is fearful
enough, but we are astounded at the fact of a
bishop of Tours, even in these times, having
burned a man alive, to obtain the deeds of an

to seek a suitable spot for a new
mission.   He founded one at Stein-
achthal, in a wild, retired spot, in 613,
where he died, between 627 and 646.
He had refused an appointment as
abbot of Luxeuil.   Thus originated

estate which he coveted.   Fredegonde, wife of
Chilperic I., one of the grandsons of Clovis,
sends two murderers to assassinate Childebert,
and these assassins are *clergymen.*   She causes
the Archbishop of Rouen to be murdered while
chanting the service in church ; and in this crime
a bishop and an archdeacon are her accomplices.
Marriage was a bond contracted and broken on
the slightest occasion.

It was into a country where all the bonds
which bind society together were totally dissolved,
that St. Columbanus flung himself with all the
headlong courage of his race, to be the cham-
pion of morals, the apostle of civilization, the
fearless soldier of the cross of Christ.   The two
languages used by him, the Celtic and the Latin,
would, of course, carry him everywhere ; and
the king eventually settled upon him the old
Roman castle of Annegray, where the first Irish
monastery ever planted on the Continent raised
its head.   There he laid the foundations of his
system as he had learned it in Ireland.   These

the famous monastery of St. Gall,
which afterwards became so eminently distinguished as the chief seat
of learning of ancient Germany.

In the seventh century many other
Irishmen followed in the footsteps of

foundations are plain, aye, the very plainest,
living, high thinking, and hard work. He lived
for weeks, according to his biographer, Jonas
of Bobio, without any other food than the herbs
of the field and the wild fruits yielded by the
forest around. We trace in him the same love of
nature and of natural objects which we find in
some of the beautiful stories told of St. Columba.
All nature seems to have obeyed his voice. The
birds came to receive his caresses. The squirrels
ran to him from the tree-tops to hide themselves in the folds of his cowl. One day, when
wandering in the depths of the woods, medi-
tating whether the ferocity of brutes, which
could not sin, was not better than the rage of
men, which destroyed their souls, he saw a
dozen wolves approach and surround him on
all sides. He remained motionless, repeating
the words, *Deus in adjutorium*. The wolves
touched his garment with their mouths, but
seeing him fearless, passed upon their way.

The example of a quiet Christian household,

Columbanus and his associates, went to France and established numerous missionary stations, which sent forth pupils, both Franks and Alemanni, capable of carrying on the work of their teachers. We have less particular information about these workers than we have of Columbanus and

shedding the blessings of civilization, education, and religion all around, proved a very powerful one, even upon men more ferocious than wolves. Crowds flocked to the Irish teacher to learn the secret of a pure and happy life, and the great foundations of Luxeuil and Fontaines followed one another in rapid succession. Among the disciples of Columbanus were numbered by hundreds the children of the noblest Franks and Burgundians. For twenty years this great missionary thus labored, till the crisis of his life came, and his activity was changed to a new direction. Having been driven from France owing to his quarrel with the wicked Queen Brunhilde, his only chance of escape was by the Rhine to Switzerland, whence, after successful labors, he painfully crossed the Alps into Italy, where he was received with great respect and endowed with the church and territory of Bobio. Columbanus undertook to restore the

his influential envoys, as related by the Abbot Jonas of Bobio. But so much is known: that near the end of the seventh century and at the beginning of the eighth, a long series of these missionary establishments extended from the mouths of the Meuse and Rhine to the Rhone and

old church of St. Peter's, which was in existence there, and to add to it a monastery. Despite his age, he shared the workmen's labors, and bent his old shoulders under the weight of enormous beams of fir-wood. This Abbey of Bobio was, in one sense, his last stage. He made it a citadel of orthodoxy against the Arians, lighting there a lamp of knowledge and instruction which long illumined Northern Italy. The monastery existed until suppressed by the French in 1803, while the church still serves as a parish church. But Columbanus ended life by seeking a solitude more profound still. Upon the opposite shore of Trebbia he discovered a cavern, which he transformed into a chapel, and there, like other Irish anchorites, he spent his last days " in solitude," till God called His faithful and fearless servant home, on November 21, 615.

At Bobio the coffin, chalice, and holly-stick or crosier of St. Columbanus are still preserved.

the Alps, while many others founded by Germans are the offspring of Irish monks, and throughout the chronicles and " Lives of the Saints," names purely Irish are constantly found: Caidor, Furseus, Fullan, Ultan, Foillan, Goban, Deicolus, and Livin are among the best authenticated names. The Merovingian king, Dagobert, retired in 656 to one of the cloisters founded by the Irish; and the so-called " Annals of Lorsch," record the dates of the deaths of a whole line of Irish abbots: Canan (704), Domnan (705), Cellan (706), Dubdecras (726), Macflathei (729), from the different monasteries.

Alcuin, the great author and the pride of Charlemagne's court, had undoubtedly these same Irish apostles in mind, when in a letter written to an Irish monk at the beginning of the eighth century he mentions the fact that in old times (*antiquo tem-*

pore) the most learned instructors of Britain, Gaul, and Upper Italy were from Ireland.

But the Irish missions had spread even to the other side of the Rhine, as well as the most eastern of the Frank settlements, and even into Bavaria, then independent of the Franks. According to the testimony of the Abbot Jonas of Bobio, contemporary of St. Columbanus, and at one time a monk in his Italian convent, as well as his biographer, about six hundred and twenty missionaries went from Luxeuil, the headquarters of Columbanus' missionary work, into Bavaria; and toward the end of that century, the Irish monk Kilian, together with his associates, Bishops Colman and Totman, suffered martyrdom at Würzburg, near the boundary of Thuringia and the country of the eastern Franks.

Ireland even shared indirectly in attempts to convert the Frieslanders and Saxons.[1] Those energetic missionaries, at the end of the seventh century, Victberct, Hewald, and Wilibrord, although Anglo-Saxons by birth, all received their theological training in Ireland. Bede's *Historia Gentis Anglorum*, book v, ix, x. Alcuin relates of Wilibrord, the Apostle to Friesland, that he spent twelve years in Ireland under the most distinguished teachers of theology. " Britain gave him birth, but Ireland reared and educated him." (*Quem tibi iam genuit fecunda Brit-*

[1] Dr. Reeves notices the achievements of the following Irish missionaries : SS. Cataldus, Fiacra, Fridolin, Colman, and Kilian, none of whom find place in English annals. St. Cataldus labored in Southern Italy ; St. Fiacra, in France ; St. Colman is patron Saint of Lower Austria ; Kilian taught in Franconia ; Fridolin, at Glarus, where his figure finds place in the cantonal arms and banner.

tania mater doctaque nutrivit studiis sed Hibernia sacris.)

From the biography of Columbanus we can get a true picture of the personal appearance of the Irish missionaries, and of their mode of procedure in their work. In groups of twelve under a leader (the abbot of the future settlement, who was generally its chieftain also), carrying long staves, leathern knapsacks, and flasks and writing tablets,[1] they travelled through the land of the Franks, with long, flowing locks and painted eyelids. They appeared thus among the Franks and Alemanni, exhorting them with fiery eloquence, at first through an interpreter, and afterwards in the language of the country, which many acquired, like Gallus (St.

[1] Their long, narrow tablets of wood were often mistaken by the unlettered natives for swords, and supposed to be in reality constructed of iron, and intended to shed blood.

Gall). Wherever they settled down, they erected within a large enclosure little wooden huts and a chapel. They supported life by cultivating the land and by fishing, and sought to influence the people of the surrounding country by exhortation, precept, and example. Both Franks and Romans joined them, and similar colonies were formed far and near from this first one as a starting-point. There is no trace of any attempt having been made here by these Irish missionaries or their German pupils to draw the heathen into the lap of Christianity by means of the external ceremony of baptism.

It is difficult for us to realize what the pagan life really was which these early Celtic missionaries had to confront, or the effect produced by their contrasted life of purity and self-denial upon the surrounding pagan masses, whose respect they com-

pelled. When the Anglo-Saxon Winfrid, surnamed Boniface, appeared in
the kingdom of the Franks as a papal legate in 723, to romanize the
existing Church of the time, not one
of the German tribes (Franks, Thu-
ringians, Alemanni) or the Bavarians
could be considered as pagans. What
Irish missionaries and their foreign
pupils had implanted for more than
a century quite independently of
Rome, Winfrid organized and established under Roman authority, partly
by force of arms.

Considering the attitude of the
Irish monks in the seventh century toward the Anglo-Saxons and
Franks, it is quite easy to compre-
hend in what way and how earnest
was the desire for knowledge awak-
ened in their converts, and why it
became a necessity for these to group
themselves around their revered instructors and to follow in their lead.

Thereupon Anglo-Saxons flocked to Ireland in large numbers to complete their education, both religious and classical, in Irish monasteries. Many such instances are quoted by Bede (672–735) in his " History of the Anglo-Saxons." He informs us that in 654, many nobles among the Angles went to Ireland to pursue theological studies, and were warmly welcomed by the Irish, who furnished them with board, instruction, and even the necessary manuscripts quite free of expense. He gives the names of two of the most conspicuous of these Angles, Edilhun and Ecgberct, as well as a brother of the former, who, after completing his studies in Ireland, returned home to conduct a bishopric. In another part of his book, Bede speaks of Victberct (above mentioned) as the pupil of Ecgberct, and quotes him as a most distinguished theologian (*doctrinæ*

scientia insignis), adding in paren-
thesis, by way of explanation evidently, that he had passed many
years in Ireland.

But the most eloquent testimony
to Ireland's fame as a seat of learning in the seventh century is furnished
us by the Anglo-Saxon Aldhelm.
Born in 850, of a noble race, he enjoyed the privilege of the instruction
of Hadrian, an abbot of Kent, who
came from Tarsos with Theodore,
Archbishop of Canterbury, and who
was considered an accomplished
Latin and Greek scholar. Aldhelm
then went to the monastery of
Malmsbury, founded by the Irish,
where he continued his studies with
great zeal. It is related of him that
he mastered Latin thoroughly, and
understood Greek equally well, beside Anglo-Saxon. Thus was the
school at Malmsbury, originally
founded by an Irish monk (Mael-

dun or Maelduf), raised by Aldhelm to become one of the noblest institutions of learning in England.

About this time, the middle of the seventh century, the Irish Church assumed a somewhat independent position toward Rome. A number of innovations had found their way from Rome into the Christian Church of the West, such as changes in the basis of calculation regarding the correct time for the celebration of Easter, questions as to the mode of wearing the tonsure,[1] the uncondi-

---

[1] The Greek tonsure, styled St. Paul's, was total ; the Roman, styled St. Peter's, was coronal. The Celtic tonsure, on the other hand, was from ear to ear ; that is, the anterior half of the head was made bare, but the middle part was untouched. Thus it was as different from the Eastern as it was from the Roman tonsure, and clearly had grown up among the Celtic Christians without any copying of other churches, Eastern or Western. — Haddan's " Remains," p. 239.

tional celibacy of the higher orders of the priesthood, etc.[1]

These were all new to the Irish Church and to the communities founded by her missionaries. Gregory the Great and his immediate

[1] " The feast of Easter has been a subject of controversy since the second century. The churches of Asia followed the Jewish method of computation, while all other churches observed the Christian style. The *earliest* Easter cycle of the Christian Church was naturally identical with that used by the Jews. It was called the eighty-four year cycle. During the debates of the second century, this cycle was discovered to be faulty, and Rome determined to have a reform of the calendar.

" But the Irish Church had received with St. Patrick and its first teachers the old Jewish and Roman cycle of eighty-four years. Barbarian invasions and wars and distance separated the Irish teachers from Rome and its new fashions. They knew nothing of the new cycle of 532 years. Their whole energy was concentrated in study and missionary effort, and so they continued faithful to the practices of their forefathers. When St. Augustine and the Roman mission came to Canterbury, about the year 600,

successors took infinite pains to establish outward uniformity in church
matters, and on Saxon soil, where
the Irish missionaries from the north
met the Romish from the south,
these differences became sharply de-
fined. The Irish were obliged out-

it was found that Rome and Ireland differed very
considerably about this important question."

The Roman Church laid the penalty of exclu-
sion from Christian communion upon all those
who would not conform themselves to her calcu-
lations, regarding them as Jews, and thus originated a most bitter and prolonged strife in the
history of the Church.

The Celtic Church finally yielded to the See
of Rome in this matter by the beginning of the
eighth century, but this consent involved no
submission in regard to other matters, so that
the Celtic Church continued to differ from Rome
on very important questions, even down to the
twelfth century.

The supremacy of Rome over Ireland would
doubtless have been established much sooner but
for the Danish invasions. Those pagan Danes
cut Ireland off from the Continent just as, three
centuries earlier, the Saxon irruption completely
isolated the British Islands.

wardly to yield their opinions on Saxon ground, and Colman was forced to leave Northumbria. It can be readily understood how fanatical partisans of Rome, such as Aldhelm, frowned upon the fact that large numbers of young Anglo-Saxons were now congregating in Ireland, and sorely feared they would return imbued with heretical views. In such a mood and under the influence of such views, Aldhelm writes from England to one of three young men just returned from Ireland:

Why does Ireland pride herself upon a sort of priority, in that such numbers of students flock there from England, as if here upon this fruitful soil there were not an abundance of Argive or Roman masters to be found, fully capable of solving the deepest problems of religion and satisfying the most ambitious of students.

But Aldhelm's reluctance to acknowledge the supremacy of the Irish monasteries is merely an additional testimony to the high degree of culture attained by them in the seventh century.[1]

But not by Anglo-Saxons alone was Ireland looked upon as the highest seminary of learning; the Franks were also at this time strongly attracted by her great fame. Bede

[1] "After the seventh century, the missionary activity of the Irish Church was no longer the one absorbing national thought and passion. Other interests had arisen. The Roman controversy about Easter, and the ever-increasing claims of the Roman See, helped to distract attention.

"Controversy then, as now, led men's minds from practical work, and hindered the advance of the Gospel. The incursions of the Danes, too, deprived the Irish Church of that internal tranquillity needful for missionary enterprise. The boldest spirits, which used to seek the post of danger and the crown of martyrdom in foreign missions, could now find that position much nearer home."

mentions a Frank named Agilberct,
who spent several years in the study
of theology in Ireland, and on leaving that country was persuaded to
remain for a time in England. On
his return to his own country, he was
made bishop of Paris, where he died
at an advanced age. But more striking than are these individual instances is the indisputable fact that
the Irish were destined to become
the instructors of the Germans,
Franks, and Alemanni in every
known department of knowledge of
that time.

As is well known, in 752 the last of
the degenerate Merovingian kings
retired to a cloister, and Pepin's energetic son Charlemagne (768–814)
greatly encouraged education among
his Frankish subjects and the German tribes he governed. His chief
architect and private secretary, Einhard or Eginhard, who wrote his

biography, tells us that such was Charlemagne's desire to perfect himself in the art of writing, that he kept a writing tablet constantly by him, and even put it under his pillow, that his right hand, grown stiff with the exercise of warlike arms, might accustom itself to form the letters.[1]

To Irish scholars France now offered a fruitful field, and Charlemagne received them with open arms. The most illustrious foreigner attached to his court was Alcuin, an Anglo-Saxon monk, and a very learn-

---

[1] "Charlemagne was, to a great extent, the founder of our modern European system of civilization. To him are largely due all our modern institutions, political, religious, and social. Art, learning, and literature are under the profoundest obligations to a prince who, though he could scarcely sign his name, and was in many respects a rude barbarian at heart, yet always displayed the keenest interest in, and sympathy with, subjects of which he was profoundly ignorant."

ed man, who became Charlemagne's chaplain and chief counsellor ; but in looking back over the latter half of his reign, and those of his immediate successors, we find the names of numerous Irish scholars. As in the early part of the seventh century, the Merovingian kings welcomed the Irish apostles who spread Christianity and the first elements of culture among the German tribes, so now in the ninth century, in schools and monasteries all over France, the Carlovingian kings employed Irish monks as teachers of writing, and tutors in grammar, logic, rhetoric, astronomy, and arithmetic.[1]

[1] The commercial intercourse between France under the Merovingian kings and Ireland was very important indeed. Dagobert Second was sent to Ireland for his education. Innumerable foreign ecclesiastics came to Ireland in that age to improve themselves in the study of Scripture, then so extensively cultivated there.

From one author of Charlemagne's time we

A friend of Alcuin, one Joseph
(*Scotus genere*), an Irishman by birth,
went to France with him before 790.
All that we know of him is that he
was employed there as a teacher, and
died before Alcuin (804). Among

learn that even Orientals sought the shelter of
this island, driven thither by the intolerance of
the Eastern emperors.

From the close and direct correspondence between the French court at that age and the lead-
ing Irish monasteries, there is no difficulty in
accounting for the transmission from Gaul to
Ireland of a type of architecture resulting in the
round towers, which have excited such interest
among archæologists,—a type eminently suited
to the troublous times of the Danish invasion.
These towers, the object of much debate, are now
pronounced to be of Christian and ecclesiastical
origin, and were erected at various periods between the fifth and thirteenth centuries. They
were undoubtedly designed to answer a twofold
use ; namely, to serve as belfries, and as keeps
or places of strength, in which the sacred uten-
sils, books, relics, and other valuables were de-
posited, and into which the ecclesiastics to whom
they belonged could retire for security in case of
sudden predatory attack. They were also prob-

the scholars of Charlemagne's court, we read in the writings of Theodulf, a Spaniard, of a certain Irish monk who lived in constant enmity with Theodulf, Angilbert, and Einhard. Theodulf attacks him with the great-

ably used when occasion required as beacons and watch-towers. The very ancient Irish churches had no bell-towers apart from the round tower. The date of the earliest is somewhat disputed by different authorities, but all agree that it precedes the invasion of the Danes. It may be argued, if the type were originally imported from France, why are such detached church towers not to be seen there still, when they are so common in Ireland? The answer to that is, that the Continental church-towers of the Carlovingian age have been almost wholly destroyed, and generally replaced by towers of a later and more beautiful type, while they have been left to stand in Ireland.

The invention of towers and steeples is traced directly back to Syria. The earliest churches were simple basilicas. The basilica was the Roman modification of the Greek temple and of Greek architecture. The Greeks knew nothing of the principle of the arch. This was the Roman contribution to the science of architec-

est virulence and contempt, and by leaving out one letter of his name, makes of Scotus either Sottus or Cottus.

To some Irishman, whose name is unknown, also patronized by Charlemagne, is attributed an epic poem, ture. Neither the Greek temple nor the Roman basilica had anything like a *tower* attached to it. It is a fact of noteworthy importance that this style of architecture came from the very same quarter whence came many other peculiarities of the early Celtic Church.

To the Eastern researches instituted by Napoleon Third we owe these interesting facts.

Another account says : " These lofty towers, undoubtedly the keeps of the monasteries, were a protection to their churches, compelled by the attempted colonization of Ireland by a pagan invader resolved to extirpate the Christianity he found there. Various towers on the Continent which bear resemblance to those of Ireland are, without doubt, of contemporary date. Such were the eleven round towers of Ravenna, of which six still remain ; that of San Nicolo of Pisa, San Paternian at Venice, Schness in Switzerland, St. Thomas in Strasburg, Gernrode in the Hartz, two at Nivelles in Belgium, one at

wrıtten in 787 to celebrate Charlemagne's victory over Thassilo, Grand Duke of Bavaria. The same " Irish exile " *(Hibernicus exul)*, as he calls himself, addressed several poems to Charlemagne as " Kaiser," by which we judge that the " Irish exile " must

St. Maurice Épinal, one at St. Germain des Prés, one at Worms in Hesse-Darmstadt, and two at Notre Dame de Maestricht in Belgium. The isolated position of Ireland on the outskirts of Europe alone accounts for the remarkable preservation of these towers from attacks of barbarians which desolated the Continent.

" They may all be said to derive their origin from an influx of Byzantine workmen into the north of Italy and to the court of Charlemagne, and the circular tower may be a reminiscence of the Eastern cylindrical pillar. Unfortunately, in France, according to Viollet le Duc, nothing but the lower stories of such towers are left, which must have existed during the Carlovingian age. The absence of such upon the Continent has led to great difficulty and obscurity in pronouncing with certainty upon the age and use of the Irish towers. Dr. Petrie, however, by his investigations brought their date down from a pre-Christian time to a period ranging from the

have been the *sobriquet* of a well-known and distinguished personage at court.

Another Irish scholar, named Clemens, is mentioned by a monk of St. Gall as arriving at Charlemagne's court near the end of the ninth century, and innumerable anecdotes are related concerning the rich and indolent pupils of his school, as well

sixth to the thirteenth century, and firmly established their ecclesiastical character.

"The inscriptions upon the high crosses of Ireland, of which there are forty-five still remaining, show that they were commemorative, as, for instance, those dedicated to the memory of Patrick and Columba. There is no evidence whatever to prove that such sculpture as we find upon these was executed before the tenth century, but the ornamentation upon various sepulchral slabs is *incised* (that upon the high crosses being in relief), which shows a knowledge of the art of modelling the human figure, and acquaintance with the early Christian Art of the Byzantine and Roman schools, and their systems of iconography. These sepulchral slabs date from

as the poor and diligent ones. Clemens was tutor to the future Emperor Lothaire, and continued his labors in the court seminary after Charlemagne's death. His fame was so great that the Abbot Ratgar of Fulda sent Modestus and some of the best pupils from the monastery of Fulda to study grammar under the Irish monk. Clemens died in Würzburg in 826, after having made a pious pilgrimage to the grave of

the seventh to the tenth century. The study of the iconography of the British Isles is of paramount interest as bearing evidence to the gradual entrance of their inhabitants into the current of European thought and culture, and their ultimate assimilation with the larger, fuller life of Continental Europe.

"Christian subjects, similar to those on the Irish stones, are found upon sarcophagi at Arles, at Ravenna, and at Velletri.

"This art of sculpture, which spread throughout Britain in the ninth and tenth centuries, attained there more beautiful results than elsewhere, owing to the fine, artistic instincts of the Celtic mind."

his fellow-countryman, the sainted Kilian. In the court records he was called "Instructor to the Imperial Court" (*magister palatinus*).

Dungal was another Irish savant who was employed by Charlemagne and his successors. He probably went to France at the same time with Clemens, and seems to have enjoyed a high reputation as an astronomer, having, at Charlemagne's suggestion, written a scientific report upon two solar eclipses which had taken place during the preceding year. He laments in the reports the want of reference books, particularly the work of Pliny the Younger, and declares it impossible to pronounce definitely upon all phases of the subject as he would wish to. During the early part of his stay in France, he lived at St. Denis; afterwards we find him in Upper Italy at the Monastery of St. Augustine, in Pavia.

where he was directed by Charlemagne to form and superintend a class of ambitious young students. By a bull, issued by Lothair the First in 823, he was appointed to a high position in the Academy at Pavia, to which pupils from Milan, Brescia, Lodi, Bergamo, Vercelli, Genoa, and Como were sent. Here in Lombardy he engaged in a controversy with Claudius (whom we have referred to above) upon questions pertaining to Church matters, and we learn, moreover, that Dungal was not only intimate with the older Christian poets such as Prudentius and Fortunatus, but also greatly esteemed Virgil and Priscian, the famous Roman grammarian. He ended his life in the monastery of Bobio, not far from Pavia, founded by his famous compatriot, Columbanus. This monastery was situated in a retired gorge in the Apennines, and its school and

library rank among the most celebrated of the Middle Ages. Its
manuscripts prove the high scholarship and deep research of the Irish
missionaries. Even modern learning
owes something to this library. We
have seen a catalogue made in the
tenth century of the manuscripts
belonging to this monastery, forty of
which are mentioned as " presented
to the monastery of St. Columbanus
by the distinguished Irish scholar,
Dungal"; and at the present day
some of these are to be seen in the
Ambrosiana, at Milan, dedicated in
Dungal's own handwriting, and in
which he speaks of himself as " belonging to " the monastery of Bobio.

Another Irish scholar, Dicuil, lived
at the Carlovingian court at the same
time with Dungal, and undoubtedly
filled a position in the same institution. Through his works we know
him as a grammarian and metrician,

as well as an astronomer and geographer. In 814–816, he produced an entirely new treatise upon astronomy, and in 825, at an advanced age, a well-known text-book of geography, for some scientific facts of which he was indebted to contemporary travellers. This book gave the first authentic information about the Faroe Islands, which had been visited by Irish hermits more than a hundred years before, but were in his time forsaken, on account of the incursions of Norman pirates. He mentions the fact of the Irish having escaped by sail-boats. Moreover, he has the first reliable information in regard to Iceland, knowledge which he obtained thirty years before from Irish priests, who remained there from February to August. The truth of these interesting accounts is proved in two ways: in the first place, the tolerably exact statements as to the length and shortness of the days could only have been determined by a resident in the place; then from Northern and independent sources we know that the first Norwegian settlers, who were, of course, pagans, found Christians there whom they called *Papar*,[1] and who left Irish books, croziers, bells, and other things behind them when they went away.

When we recall the Irish missions established on the Continent, and the fact that St. Kataldus, the patron saint of Tarento, in Southern Italy, was an Irish pilgrim of the seventh century, and that Irishmen went to the Faroe Islands at the same time,

[1] The Irish anchorites found in Iceland by the heathen colonists were called *Papar*, from *papa*, meaning priest or pope. This derivation, however, may be considered as somewhat doubtful, for their whole history is involved in obscurity. The islands of Papey on the southern coast of Iceland, also Papey in Orkney and other places, are supposed to be named after them.

and to Iceland in the eighth century,
we can realize the extent and strength
of the nomadic instinct or impulse
which drove those Irish Christians
out into the unknown world to open
its eyes to the light of Christianity.
How strongly the Alemanni of the
ninth century, who never left their
own country, were impressed by this
trait of the Irish, is perceived by the
well-known remark of Walahfrid
Strabo (849), when, in allusion to
them, he says : "The habit of rambling to distant lands has become a
second nature to this people."

Equal to Dicuil as to the extent
of his general knowledge, but far
surpassing him in originality of
thought, was his compatriot Johannes Scotus Erigena. The greatest
thinker of his age, his philosophical
works mark an epoch in the world's
literature, in the opinion of many
modern critics. Of the particulars

of his career, we know scarcely more than that he was living in the kingdom of the Franks in '840, and received a position in the court school, under that generous patron of science, Charles the Bald; that he in time became principal of the school, and was still living in 877. He is distinguished both from his predecessors and from those who came after him, by not having taken orders; and, although educated in a monastery, was the first layman who had excelled in scholarship for a long period. In his knowledge of Greek, particularly of the Greek fathers and philosophers, he far surpassed all other scholars. He was ordered by Charles the Bald to translate into Latin the works of Dionysius Areopagita, in which a sort of Neoplatonism, modified by Christianity, is expounded. His *chef-d'œuvre* is, however, his "System of Philosophy" produced before 865 (περὶ φυσεως μερισμοῦ, *id est, De divisione naturæ*), in which he had the hardihood to present philosophy as an independent science, and of equal importance with theology, which, as he affirmed, is supported by authority, as philosophy by reason. Authority (or Holy Writ) is to theology what nature is to reason. Where the two come in collision, reason must take the lead; for it needs not the support of authority. These aphorisms of Erigena's were so astounding for that time that it is not to be wondered at that he, as a layman, was considered as encroaching upon the subject of predestination, then being contested in the Church, and that his writings were condemned on all sides. He became involved in dogmatic controversies, and was cried down on every side as a heretic. Pope Nicholas I. demanded of Charles the Bald Erigena's presence in Rome, that he might vindicate himself; but Charles the Bald esteemed the philosopher too highly to let him go, and he remained unmolested. Erigena's work was, however, condemned by several church councils and finally at Rome in 1059. Beside a commentary on Marcianus Capella, he wrote a number of occasional poems, dedicated to his royal patron on certain festal days, as well as several in the Greek language.

Contemporary with Johannes Scotus Erigena, we find another able Irish scholar working in France— Sedulius Scotus. As we learn from one of his poems, he reached the cathedral chapter house, at Liège, one intensely cold day, through deep snow drifts, exhausted by hunger and fatigue, and was warmly welcomed on account of his classical attainments. He was employed there as teacher from 840 to 860, and soon

after died at Milan. He was pro-
ficient in mythology and ancient history, a finished Latin scholar, and
familiar with Greek. Beside commentaries on the Holy Scriptures
and grammatical treatises, which
were a necessary part of the education of every scholar of that time,
he composed numerous poems, for
special occasions, addressed to Charles
the Bald, whose praises he sang when
that monarch visited Liège, drawn
thither by the literary fame of its
monastery. A comic poem is also
attributed to Sedulius. A bishop
had presented him with a sheep. A
thief stole it, and, being chased by
dogs, dropped his prey, which naturally was seized upon by the dogs.
The victim's heroic resistance against
terrible odds is graphically described
by the bard. From the poems of
Sedulius, we learn that many of his
countrymen, "learned grammarians,"

were also at Liège, one of whom, Cruindmel, left behind him a grammatical treatise of importance.[1]

But Irish scholars were also laboring among the Eastern Franks, the Bavarians and Alemanni. One of them, named Virgil, was bishop of Salzburg from 743 to 784. He had been abbot of Aghaboe in Ireland, but, on going to France, was recommended, by Pepin, to Odilo, Grand Duke of Bavaria, to fill the See of Salzburg. In the year 740, the papal legate, Bonifatius, denounced him at Rome for promulgating false doctrines, as he maintained that the sun and moon passed underneath the earth, and that there must be inhabitants on the other side. This accusation shows that Virgil must have been conversant with Greek litera-

[1] " At Vienna there is a copy of the 'Life of St. Columba,' being a manuscript of Sedulius, written in double columns, with red initial letters."

ture, and probably familiar with the doctrine of Eudoxus and Eratosthenes, as to the spherical form of the earth. Irish annals give him the surname of the "geometrician."

Dobda, or Dobdagrecus, a compatriot of Virgil, possibly so called from his knowledge of Greek, was also a teacher at Salzburg, but *Dobdagrecus* is probably a Latin form of the word Dubdachrich, a name often quoted in Irish annals of the time, as having distinguished himself in Bavaria as a teacher.

In the German monastery of Rheinau, a few miles beyond Schaffhausen, we find, in the ninth century, an account of an illustrious Irishman, Findan, who, though no representative of Irish scholarship, may be cited here as a famous character of mediæval times. He was a native of Leinster, and in 840 went with several companions on pilgrim-

ages through Gaul, Alemannia, and
Lombardy.   After being a priest for
four years among the Alemanni, he
retired in 851 to the Rheinau monastery, and died there in 878.   For
the last twenty-two years of his re-
tirement at Rheinau, he, of his own
free will, endured the severest pen-
ances and privations, which greatly
added to the monastery's renown.
His voluntary sacrifices were at first
beyond his power of endurance; the
spirit was too weak to resist the
cravings of a devouring hunger.
Then he had recourse to prayer; he
saw visions and heard celestial voices,
which counselled and exhorted him
in an ancient Irish dialect, although
he was in the far distant land of the
Alemanni.   Now the oldest of the
manuscripts, which give us those
Irish phrases uttered by heavenly
voices, date only from the tenth century, and must have been noted

down directly after Findan's death. and in the handwriting of one of his fellow-countrymen. The voices exhorted him to patience, whereupon his temptation passed from him. The picture of an Irish pilgrim in Alemannia, wrestling with earthly longings, and supported by voices from heaven, which spoke in the ancient Irish tongue, is certainly an original one. Since the *Vita* could evidently only have been written out by some one familiar with the Irish language, it is proved that near Findan's time, as well as later, Irish promoters of learning were settled on that island in the Rhine.

In the neighboring monastery of Reichenau *(augia major)*, on an island in Lake Constance, we find traces of Irish culture, if not of Irish monks themselves. In alluding to the German abbot, Erlebald, of noble birth (822–838), his successor,

Walahfrid Strabo (849), says that the former was first instructed in theology at Reichenau, by Heito, and afterwards was sent with a companion to some learned Irish instructor, to enjoy the privilege of his training in secular branches of science and the arts. We find that at the same time, Ratgar of Fulda sent scholarly monks for the same object to the Irish Clemens, the director of the school, which makes it quite probable that Clemens was also the instructor of Erlebald. While Erlebald was abbot, a catalogue of the library at Reichenau was made. It consisted of 415 manuscripts, 30 of which were written in the cloister in Erlebald's time (822–838). Seven of these volumes were presented by him from his own private library.

Considering that Irish monks were at Rheinau in the ninth century, and had, as we find, much intercourse with those of St. Gall, it is strange that we have no positive proof of their presence in Reichenau, it being situated on one of the most frequented and direct routes to Rome. This fact is the more remarkable, inasmuch as we have at the present day a large quantity of manuscripts, dating from the end of the eighth into the ninth century, from the library of Reichenau, which were undoubtedly written by Irish savants, as for example: at St Paul, in Lavanthale (Steyermark), there is a manuscript full of extracts written by some Irish monk, and brought from St. Blasien one hundred years ago, which contains Irish poems dating from the end of the eighth century, Latin hymns, the commencement of a commentary on Virgil, a treatise on astronomy, Greek declinations and paradigms, as well as a

short Greek vocabulary. In Carlsruhe, there is a manuscript from
Reichenau,. together with several
works of Bede, dating from the first
half of the ninth century, which
must have been written in Ireland,
chronological notes and explana-
tions of the text being the work of
three different Irishmen and one
German.   There is also in Carlsruhe
a manuscript of Priscian, of the same
date as the above, which not only
gives the so-called Irish recension of
this author, but contains Irish comments as well.

Now the question arises how these
manuscripts and others written by
Irishmen, could have been found at
Reichenau. Ekkehard the Younger,
the chronicler of St. Gall, informs us
that at the time of the Magyar invasion of 925, the books from the
monastery of St. Gall were trans-
ported to Reichenau for safety, and

that when all danger was over the same number were returned, but not the same manuscripts. Unless we have recourse to the highly improbable assumption that *all* the manuscripts at Reichenau of Irish origin are owing to that interchange, it follows that we must concede the fact that there must have been Irish teachers there in the ninth century. Among the books added to the library at Reichenau under Erlebald (823–838), is mentioned a *Prisciani de arte grammaticæ liber unus quem Uragrat presbyter dedit;* this must be the noted Irish version of Priscian.

St. Gall [1] was the most celebrated monastery in Germany at that time, and for more than three hundred years it was looked upon as the

[1] The quadrangular bell of St. Gallus is preserved in the monastery of St. Gall. There is also a silver book-shrine (in the museum) of Irish workmanship. Gallus was the favorite and most honored disciple of Columbanus.

chief nursery of learning of the whole kingdom. It owes its reputation greatly to its connections with Ireland and the work of learned Irish monks in its university. For Irish travellers to that region, it must always be an attractive spot, as having been founded in 613 by their compatriot, the learned monk Gallus. Although the annals of this monastery, absorbed apparently with accounts of its external prosperity, make no mention of these relations with Ireland until the early part of the ninth century, so much the more striking become other more genuine proofs. In Ireland, during the sixth and seventh centuries, a considerable change is perceptible in the writing of the Latin manuscripts, as to the form of several letters and otherwise, showing a marked difference to the Latin of the Continent, particularly that of France and Italy. Now the so-called *Vocabularius S. Galli* was written in 780, in the Irish method of writing Latin, a sure proof of the presence of learned Irish monks in St. Gall at that time. There is still to be seen there a written catalogue compiled in the first half of the ninth century, reporting not less than twenty volumes *(volumina)*, two smaller ones *(codicilli),* and nine other manuscripts in the Irish Latin,—a testimony which speaks louder than the ordinary, insufficient chronicle of a monastery. In one of the manuscripts the removal of the bones of St. Gall to the new church is narrated (835); there were, therefore, Irish eye-witnesses to that event in the monastery at the time, and the catalogue is of a later date.

We find other external proofs of the residence of Irish monks at St. Gall and of the efficiency of their instruction there. Walahfrid Strabo, in his revision of Gozbert's account of the miracles of St. Gall, mentions the miraculous cure of a sick Irishman left behind by his travelling companions, who was still living in the monastery after his recovery, in the writer's day,—a furthur proof of Irish visitors and residents at St. Gall in the first half of the ninth century.

At about the same time that Johannes Scotus Erigena was directing the school at Paris, Sedulius Scotus devoting himself to teaching in the cathedral school at Liège, and Findan at the monastery of Rheinau, there came to St. Gall, on their return from Rome, an Irish bishop named Marcus and his nephew, Moengal, with a number of compatriots. Moengal, afterwards in the monastery called Marcellus, or "the little Marcus," seems to have made a powerful impression upon the monks by his great learning, both in theology and the secular sciences, *(erat in divinis et humanis eruditissimus)*. They prevailed upon Marcus and his nephew to remain with them, with a part of their company. The rest went home laden with gifts, but their manuscripts were kept back by Marcus for his own use and for that of the monastery. Moengal must have labored for more than ten years in the school, as we have seen documents of his, bearing various dates, and he is mentioned as still living in the year 865. Ekkehard writes enthusiastically of the "great prosperity of the monastery under such favorable auspices." What Moengal achieved there can hardly indeed be overrated. The three scholars, Notker, Ratpert, and Tuotilo, were put under his instruction, after having been tutored in theology by Iso. Moengal excelled in theology as well as in every other branch of knowledge, and trained his pupils thoroughly in music. Under his teaching St. Gall was at the height of its fame. Ratpert tells us that under Abbot Grimald, 854–872, the library acquired seventy additional manuscripts, besides Grimald's gift of thirty-five more from his own private library. Moengal's residence at St. Gall produced an unwonted impetus to composition among the inmates of the monastery.

During that century, the Irish particularly excelled in two of the arts: calligraphy and music. With the first, miniature painting and sculpture were closely allied. In these the Irish show a lack of taste in representing figurative designs, combined with a high degree of *technique*, and in the art of coloring they were quite unapproachable. But the great proficiency of the Irish in calligraphy, miniature painting, and sculpture is so universally acknowledged, that further mention of the fact is superfluous.

Is it by pure accident that St. Gall is so celebrated for the beauty of its penmanship, its miniatures and carvings? Was it by chance that the two most conspicuous students of these sister arts, Sintram and Tuotilo, whose fame spread beyond the land of the Alemanni to Metz and Fulda, became pupils of Moengal? We have proofs that the Irish have been highly cultivated in music from the early mediæval times up to our own. Sedulius Scotus, teacher at the cathedral school at Liège, compares himself to Orpheus, and calls Calliope his consort.[1] Moengal gave

[1] The arts in which Christian Ireland excelled before the thirteenth century were the writing and ornamentation of MSS., metal-work, stone-cutting, and building. The first art, that of the scribe, was indeed carried to marvellous perfection in Ireland; and although, owing to the

music the highest place among the arts, and the music school of St. Gall certainly reached its fullest perfection under his three students, Ratpert, Notker, and Tuotilo.

In my opinion there were very few men who, in the middle of the ninth

invention of printing, this is no longer an honored handicraft, yet the story of the circle of Giotto shows how important technical skill was considered in the days of great religious art. "When the messenger of Pope Benedict IX. came to Florence, he requested Giotto to give him a drawing to send to his Holiness as a sample of his powers. Giotto, who was very courteous, took a sheet of paper and a pencil dipped in a red color; then, resting his elbow on his side, with one turn of his hand he drew a circle, so perfect and exact that it was a marvel to behold." To draw a perfect circle, unaided by the compasses, is a feat only to be accomplished by an eye and hand in perfect training and obedience to the artist's will. Such circles are to be seen in every page of the famous "Book of Kells," the finest amo⟩g the MSS. of the Gospels. The church of Kells, in which this book was used, was founded by Columba. There is no instance of a letter O, in the large round

century exerted such a beneficent influence upon the German mind in the cultivation of the higher arts and sciences as Moengal and his followers. I need hardly point out how little Scheffel's picture corresponds with the historic Moengal.

lettering of this book, in which the slightest sign of a swerving hand is perceptible.

"Writing," says Dr. Reeves, "formed a most important part of the monastic occupations." Besides the supply of service-books for the numerous churches that sprang into existence, and which probably were without embellishment, great labor was bestowed upon the ornamentation of some manuscripts, epecially the sacred writings ; these are wonderful monuments of the conceptions, skill, and patience of the scribes of the seventh century. The penmanship of the Irish scribes is known to have exercised a considerable influence on that of the Continent from the time of its first introduction by the Irish missionaries, and this continued to prevail till the thirteenth and fourteenth centuries. The Irish monks instructed their disciples in the technicalities of this art, such as the manner of holding the pen, the preparation of ink, and indeed the whole process of writing, the results of which

For more than a century after Moengal's time, various Irish scholars established themselves at St. Gall, as is proved by the records of deaths, which comprise very many

are of exquisite beauty. The writing apparatus consisted of *tabulæ* or waxen tablets, *graphia* or styles, *calami* or pens, made either of goose-quills or crow-quills, and the ink used was carbonaceous, not mineral. The parchment, as compared with that made use of in France from the seventh till the tenth century, was for the most part much thicker. It is often finely polished, but sometimes horny and dirty. On the whole, these scribes do not appear to have attained much perfection in the preparation of the skins, with which they were supplied by their goats, sheep, and calves. The thick ink in use is remarkable for its blackness and durability. The scarlet ink was particularly brilliant and permanent ; it was made from cockles, " a most beautiful color, which never fades with the heat of the sun or the washing of the rain, but the older it is, the more beautiful it becomes," according to Bede. He also notes that such virtue lay in the books of the Irish missionaries that the mere " scrapings of their leaves that were brought out of Ireland, if put into water and swallowed,

genuine Irish names. The tenth century was an unfortunate one for St. Gall, not to mention the seizure of the monastery by the Magyars in 925, at the time of their disastrous

were an antidote to the poison of serpents." The extraordinary neatness of the handwriting, and its firm character, have led several English antiquaries to express opinions as to the writing instruments which were used by the Irish monks. The notion that they employed extremely sharp metallic pens is quite untenable. That these were made from neither reeds nor metal, but of the quills of swans, geese, crows, and other birds, is proved by several pictures in Irish manuscripts, where the Evangelist, engaged in writing his Gospel, holds in his hand a pen, the feather of which can be clearly perceived. The ink-stand is also represented as a simple, slender, conical cup, fastened either to the arm of the chair, or upon a small stick on the ground.

Sixty-one remarkable scribes are mentioned as having flourished in Ireland before the year 900, forty of whom lived between A.D. 700 and 800.

Diligence in writing was one characteristic of St. Columba as well as of his successor at Iona, and the title of *scribe* is frequently used to enhance the dignity of a bishop.

incursions in the Rhine valley. About the year 1000 began the " Silver Age " of St. Gall, according to one of its historians, but many names which greatly contributed to its glory and reputation are in the list of those who fell victims to the plague in 1022 (Notker, Rudpert, Arno, Erimbert).

The fame of the old monastery was so increased by the brilliancy of its native scholars who, in time, far outstripped their Irish teachers, that it is hardly to be wondered at that the former began gradually to look down with a degree of contempt, possibly tinged with jealousy, upon the Irish scholars, who continued, however, to come there from time to time, the native students being inclined to forget to whom they owed the foundation of their institution. Dubwin, the Irish savant, bitterly complains of his German brethren,

reproaching them not only for appropriating to themselves the harvest
sown by others, but for assuming all
the credit of it.

It seems hardly necessary to accu-
mulate any further testimony on the
subject, after studying this long list of
Irish scholars who labored in France
under Charlemagne, his son and
grandson, to implant on German soil
a knowledge of Christian and secular
science, emanating at that time from
Ireland alone of the whole Western
world, and establishing itself at so
many different points: Clemens,
Dicuil, and Johannes Scotus Erigena at the court school; Dungal
at Pavia; Sedulius Scotus at Liège;
Virgil at Salzburg; and Moengal
at St. Gall. However, two more most
convincing proofs may be mentioned.

Hieric, in his biography of St.
Germanus, a bishop of Roman Gaul,
a work finished in the year 876, takes

occasion in his dedication of it, to laud the emperor, Charles the Bald, as the protector of Johannes Scotus Erigena against the pope, and as a promoter of general literature and of philosophical studies. After citing the fact that the emperor even summoned Greeks to his court, he exclaims:

" Need I remind Ireland that she sent troops of philosophers over land and sea to our distant shores, that her most learned sons offered their gifts of wisdom, of their own free will, in the service of our learned King, our Solomon!" One more testimony. A distinguished writer, still living, in a work on the literature of the Carlovingian period, speaks of the famous philosopher, Johannes Scotus Erigena, as having been appreciated on account of his Irish birth and education, and notably for his knowledge of Greek. The mere fact that a scholar was living in France in the middle of the ninth century, who understood Greek, and other general literature as well, was enough to arouse the idea that he must have enjoyed the privilege of Irish training, and is no insignificant testimony to Irish culture.

I have endeavored to give a detailed sketch of those Irish missionaries who came into the Merovingian kingdom of the Franks, at the beginning of the seventh century, to introduce Christianity to the German races. Some of the monks of St. Gall present quite a different picture of the Irish scholars who appeared in the Carlovingian kingdom toward the end of the eighth and in the ninth centuries. But their accounts contain many false statements as well as anachronisms, and show occasionally a spirit of jealousy and exaggeration, especially in regard to the Irish scholars' estimate of themselves and the abilities of their German pupils. However highly we estimate the work of the Irish monks in the Carlovingian period, and their claim to having been the means of introducing spiritual culture among the German and Roman peoples, we can hardly wonder that their contemporaries often expressed different opinions from ours. In many instances these foreigners were rivals of the native scholars, even if superior to them ; this would weigh heavily against them, and, moreover, they cannot be charged with an overweening modesty. We even hear of bitter enmities between the rival scholars of different nationalities in Charlemagne's court, and we read complaints of the Irish monk, Dubwin, in the eleventh century, who accuses the Frankish monks of looking down upon his fellow-laborers.

We have certain proofs of open hostilities within the cloisters. Marianus Scotus, who lived from 1056 to 1082 in various monasteries, Cologne, Fulda, and Mayence, alludes to them in his "Chronicles of the World," which can be seen in the Vatican library at Rome, being among the manuscripts stolen from the Heidelberg library. Another manuscript, written in a mixture of Irish and Latin by some other Irish student in Mayence, gives numerous foot-notes on personal matters and every-day incidents of cloister life.

Ireland's mission on the Continent, at least in all her important fields of labor, was completed in the eleventh century. But Irish monks continued to wander through the Rhine valley for a hundred years afterward, no longer, however, as apostles and teachers to the Germans. Their innate love of wandering drove

them into foreign lands to end their
lives as anchorites in various cloisters.
We read of another Irish Columbanus at Ghent in 957 ; in Cologne,
in 975, the monastery of St. Martin
was given up to Irish monks,
and, for a time, that of St. Panta-
leon was also directed by a Scotch
abbot. At about the same time
Irish monks come into possession of a monastery at Metz, where
Fingan became abbot, and where he
died in 1003 ; the hermit, Animchad,
died at Fulda in 1043, and an Irish
recluse named Paternus was buried
at Paderborn in 1058. In 1056,
Marianus Scotus left Ireland for Cologne, then went to Paderborn and
Fulda, and made a pilgrimage to
Würzburg, the resting - place of
Kilian's remains. He afterwards
lived in the monastery of Fulda as
an anchorite for ten years, then went
to Mayence, where he died in 1082,

after completing his great " Chronicle of the World " (before mentioned). The Irish savant, David, directed the cathedral school in Würzburg toward the end of the century, and became chaplain and court historian to the Emperor Henry V., whom he accompanied to Rome in 1110, then returned to Ireland to occupy a bishopric there.[1]

At the very time that traces of Irish missionary work became less and less marked in those localities which had been the scenes of their

[1] At Würzburg we find a remarkable monument of early Irish occupation in the copy of the Pauline Epistles, with the interlinear glosses. Here also is preserved the Latin Bible, which was found in Kilian's tomb in the year 743, Kilian having been interred in 687. This book is still exposed upon the altar of the cathedral church on St. Kilian's festive day. A curious representation of the crucifixion appears in this manuscript, where cherubim are ministering to the penitent thief, whilst ill-omened birds are pecking at the impenitent sinner.

most active labors from the seventh
to the tenth century, some Irish
monks succeeded in establishing
themselves in another part of Germany, where they founded an institution that became the mother of
numerous lesser monasteries which
flourished for more than a century.[1]

[1] One of the most celebrated Irish scholars
and writers of the Middle Ages was Marianus
Scotus of Ratisbon. He was an enclosed anchorite, and tells us himself that he daily said mass
standing on the grave of his predecessor, and
with his own grave open beside him. The institution of anchorites flourished to such an extent
that a rule was drawn out for them, which gives
the details of their existence. "An anchorite's
cell should be built of stone, twelve feet long,
and twelve broad. It should have three win-
dows, one facing the choir, through which he
may receive his food, and a third for light. The
window for food should be secured by a bolt and
have a glazed lattice, to be opened and shut, because no one should be able to look in except as
far as glass will allow ; nor should the anchorite
have a view out. He should be provided with
three articles, a jar, a towel, and a cup. After

In 1067 Muiredach Mac Robertaig,
generally called by his Latin name

tierce he is to lay the jar and cup outside the
window and then close it. About noon he is to
come over and see if his dinner is there. If it
be, he is to sit at the window and eat and drink.
When he has done, whatever remains is to be
left outside for any one who may choose to re-
move it, and he is to take no thought for the
morrow. But if it should happen that he has
nothing for his dinner he is not to omit his
accustomed thanks to God, though he is to remain without food till the following day. His
garments are to be a gown and cap which he is
to wear waking and sleeping. In winter he may,
if the weather be severe, wear a woolly cloak,
because he is not allowed to have any fire save
what his candle produces."

It is only of late years that facts have come to
light which alone will explain many Oriental
ideas, the existence of which in the West has
puzzled historical students. These facts explain
some peculiarities of the Celtic Church and of
Celtic monasticism. In Gaul, Syrian and Eastern
monasticism was flourishing when Christianity
passed over to Ireland. In Irish monasticism
we should therefore expect to find traces of
Syrian and Oriental practices in the constitution,
the customs, the learning, the art, and the archi-

of Marianus Scotus, started with two
associates from the north of Ireland
tecture of the early Celtic Church.   Some peculiarities of Irish monasticism, for instance, can
only be explained by a reference to Syrian ideas
and customs.   Now this anchorite institution was
a peculiar mark of Eastern monasticism.   In the
West, it took a more practical turn, the monks
being the great civilizers of the Middle Ages.
But in Ireland we find the enclosed anchorite
flourishing side by side with the agricultural or
learned and artistic monk.   Anchorites of this
kind were imported from Syria to Gaul and
thence to Ireland, where this institution flourished in greatest vigor, because it just fell in with
that tendency to extremes which ever marks the
Celtic race.   The type of the early Celtic monastery is to be sought not among the Latins, but
among the Greeks and Orientals.

Modern investigation has conclusively proved
that the Celtic race is endowed with a marvellous
tenacity, its race customs, its tribal organizations,
its tribes and traditions all embodying ideas
brought from the most distant East.

Another account says : " The most important
Irish settlement in Bavaria was at Ratisbon ; a
monastery founded there dedicated to St. James
was the parent of many Scotic monasteries.   The
' Life of the Holy Marianus Scotus of Donegal '

on a pilgrimage to Rome. After
long sojourns at various points, they

is preserved here, also his 'Commentary on the
Psalms of David.' On reaching Ratisbon, Marianus and his companions were received into the
convent of Obermünster, where Marianus was
employed by the Abbess Emma in the transcrip-
tion of books. He wrote some missals and a
number of other religious books, his companions
preparing the membranes for his use. After
some time he was minded to continue his original
journey; but a brother Irishman, called Murtagh, who was then living as a recluse at the
Obermünster, urged him to let it be determined
by Divine guidance whether he should proceed
on his way or settle for life at Ratisbon. He
passed the night in Murtagh's cell, and in the
hours of darkness it was intimated to him that
wherever on the next day he should first behold
the rising sun, he should remain and fix his
abode. Starting before day he entered St. Peter's
Church, outside the walls, to implore the Divine
blessing on his journey. But scarcely had he
come forth, when he beheld the sun stealing
above the horizon. 'Here, then,' said he, 'I
shall rest, and here shall be my resurrection.'
His determination was hailed with joy by the
whole population."

It is further recorded of Marianus that " this

reached Ratisbon, where they received a hospitable welcome at the
holy man wrote from beginning to end, with his own hand, the Old and New Testament, with explanatory comments on the same books, and that not once or twice, but over and over again, with a view to the eternal reward, all the while clad in snowy garb, living on slender diet, attended and aided by his brethren, who prepared the parchments for his use ; he wrote also many smaller books and manuals, psalters for distressed widows and poor clerics of the same city, towards the health of his soul, without any prospect of earthly gain. Furthermore, through the grace of God, many congregations of the monastic order, which in faith and charity and imitation of the blessed Marianus, are derived from the aforesaid Ireland, and inhabit Bavaria and Franconia, are sustained by the writings of the blessed Marianus." He died on the 9th of February, 1088. Aventinus, the Bavarian annalist, styles him : *Poeta et Theologus insignis, nullique suo seculo secundus.* A copy of the Epistles of St. Paul, written by Marianus " for his pilgrim brethren," is preserved in the Imperial library of Vienna. At the end of the MS. are these words : *In honore Individuæ Trinitatis, Marianus Scotus scripsit hunc librum suis fratribus peregrinis. Anima.*

Obermünster nunnery.[1] They decided to settle at Ratisbon, and founded an Irish monastery in the year 1076. Tidings of this, according to the statement of Marianus' biographer, reached Ireland, whereupon many of his countrymen left kith and kin to follow Marianus, seven of whose immediate successors to the dignity of abbot were natives of the north of Ireland. The old

ejus requiescat in pace, propter Deum devote dicite Amen.

An old chronicle says : " Now be it known, that neither before nor since was there a more noble monastery, such magnificent towers, walls, pillars, and roofs, so rapidly erected, so perfectly finished, as in this monastery, because of the wealth and money sent by the king and princess of Ireland."

" The richly decorated portal of the church escaped fire and stood out firmly against every assault."

[1] The abbesses of the nunnery of Obermünster held the rank of princesses of the Empire, and occupied seats in the Diet.

monastery soon became insufficient
for them, and they founded another,
the monastery of St. James, the
church of which was consecrated
in 1111.

But Ratisbon was by no means
the goal of these Irish monks, im-
pelled as they were by the rambling
instincts of their race. Johannes,
one of Marianus' associates, went to
Göttweich,[1] in Austria, where he
died as anchorite ; the other went to
Jerusalem. Another of Marianus'
followers went with some Ratisbon
merchants to Kief, whence they returned to the monastery, laden with
costly gifts of skins and furs. From
the proceeds of the sale of these

[1] The celebrated Benedictine monastery of
Göttweich, in Lower Austria, about forty miles
west of Vienna, was founded in 1072. It was
situated upon a steep hill, and was richly endowed. The buildings were destroyed by fire
in 1718, and afterwards rebuilt. It now belongs
to the diocese of the archbishopric of Vienna.

goods the monastery of St. James was erected, and the church already built was furnished with a new roof. On Frederick Barbarossa's return from his crusade in 1189 through the country which is now Bulgaria, he found at Skribentium a monastery governed by an Irish abbot. Letters written by Irish abbots in Ratisbon in 1090 petition King Wratislaw[1] of Bohemia for an escort for their messengers through that country to Poland. Whence it is no matter of wonderment that there arose in the twelfth century, more or less directly inspired by this influential monastery of St. James of Ratisbon,[2] a long list

---

[1] Duke Wratislaw of Bohemia was crowned king for his services to the Empire, and particularly for having sustained the Emperor Henry IV. against Rudolph, his competitor. He was rewarded with the title of king in 1086, and the hand of the emperor's daughter Julia, beside the sovereignty of Lusace. He died in 1092.

[2] St. James of Ratisbon was the last remaining

of Irish monasteries, as follows: one at Würzburg, in 1134; at Nuremberg, in 1140; at Constance, in 1142; St. George at Vienna, in 1155; at Eichstadt, in 1183; and that of St. Mary at Vienna, in 1200.

At the Lateran Council, in 1215, the twelve existing Irish monasteries of Germany were formally placed under the authority of that of St. James at Ratisbon, which received in 1225, through the favor of the Roman king, Henry, the privilege of bearing the imperial half-eagle on its escutcheon. The Abbot of St.

of the Irish-Scotch monasteries in Germany. It was closed in 1860, for want of funds to support the small number of resident monks and students. The church was built in 1100. The singular projecting north porch dates from the thirteenth century, its large circular arch (pure Norman) is supported by pillars with lions at their bases, and curiously ornamented with quaint carvings of crocodiles and other monsters, supposed to represent the triumph of Christianity over heathenism (see frontispiece).

James of Ratisbon, at this, the time
of that monastery's greatest prosperity, controlled the Irish monasteries of Oels in Silesia, Erfurt in
Thuringia, Würzburg, Nuremberg,
Eichstadt in Franconia,[1] Memmin-
gen and Constance in Swabia, and
Vienna in Austria.

The Irish monks who, from the
eleventh to the thirteenth centuries
quitted the north of Ireland to make
pilgrimages to this part of Germany,
were worthy successors of those apostles and scholars we find in France
from the seventh to the tenth centuries—full of zeal, piety, sobriety,
and a genuine love for learning. The
hospitable reception which Marianus

[1] Franconia, which lay in early times on both
sides of the Rhine (kingdom of the Franks).
is now situated south of Thuringia. The MSS.
discovered and acquired from this region were
but a small installment in discharge of the old
debt Franconia owed to Ireland for her missionary services.

Scotus found at the nunnery at Ratisbon gives evidence that he must have made himself very useful there in transcribing breviaries and other pious documents; in fact, Aventinus[1] makes mention of a psalter he himself saw at Ratisbon, which was written by Marianus for the Abbess Matilda, in the year 1074. Moreover, a chronicle of the monastery of Ratisbon, written in 1185, states that the greater portion of all the

[1] Aventinus (1460), a celebrated philologist of Bavaria, and professor of languages at Vienna and Cracow, was made tutor to the children of the Duke of Bavaria, and wrote the "Annals of Bavaria." He was imprisoned in 1529, on suspicion of heresy, but no charge was made against him, and he was released by his patron. At the age of sixty-four, he first began to contemplate marriage. He consulted his Bible, and determined to marry the first woman he met, which proved to be his own maid-servant, who was deformed, poor, and ill-tempered. He died in 1534, aged sixty-eight, and was buried in the church of St. Emmeran, at Ratisbon.

existing documents belonging to the
different Irish monasteries, which
sprang from that of St. James of
Ratisbon, were written by Marianus.
A specimen of his beautiful script
and a proof of the remarkable rapid-
ity of his work may be seen at the
court library at Vienna, where is
preserved a copy of the Epistles of
St. Paul (Codex 1247); it consists
of 160 sheets, and was written by
him between the 23d of March and
the 17th of May, 1079, as is proved
by numerous foot-notes of his own.
Very many of the monks coming
directly from monasteries in Ireland
brought books with them, which they
presented to the German monasteries.
These men (Malachias, Patricius,
Maclan, Finnian) and others (1190
to 1240) were well known to the
Irish monks in Vienna, as well as
the books themselves.

In a manuscript to be found at

Dublin, written in the Irish dialect in 1100, it is stated that a manuscript belonging to the celebrated monastery of Monasterboice, in Ulster, which had been in its possession so late as the year 1050, was missing, a student of the monastery having carried it away with him to the Continent. It was from that part of Ireland that those compatriots of Marianus Scotus came, who followed him to Ratisbon after 1076.

The chronicles of the Ratisbon monastery state that the first Irish abbot of Würzburg, Macarius (McCarthy ?) was remarkably learned in the science of theology and renowned throughout Ireland for his exhaustive study of the liberal arts. His second successor, Carus, became chaplain to Conrad III. and first abbot of the Irish monastery at Nuremberg. The next one, Declan, was chaplain both to Conrad III. and Frederic Barbarossa.

The twelfth century, that in which the basilica of St. James of Ratisbon was erected, was the most flourishing period of the Irish monks in Germany. The decline of their influence began about the middle of the thirteenth century, and is easily explained. We should make a marked distinction between these Irish monks of the eleventh, twelfth, and thirteenth centuries and those apostles sent forth from Ireland during the four previous centuries.

Columbanus and his successors set forth to preach the gospel to heathen Germany; they founded missionary stations there, and made every effort to attract the people into their midst. Their highest aim was so thoroughly to educate their pupils, both Franks and Alemanni, in the principles of Christianity, that their own presence should become superfluous; so that, in many instances, the second generation of monks in one of these institutions would be wholly German, and governed by a German abbot. It was quite otherwise with Marianus and his successors. They founded Benedictine monasteries, which were entirely closed to Germans, and continually strengthened by reinforcements from abroad. What they accomplished was neither more nor less than what any of the monasteries of German origin did.

Still less can they be compared with those champions of the Irish culture in the Carlovingian period in France. Dungal, Johannes Scotus Erigena, Clemens, Sedulius Scotus, and Moengal are representatives of a higher culture than was then to be found on the Continent: a purely Christian training and severely simple habit of mind, joined to the highest theoretical attainments based upon a thorough knowledge of the best standards of classical antiquity. These Irishmen had a high mission entrusted to them, and they faithfully accomplished their task. Marianus Scotus, and the most learned of his followers and compatriots were merely Benedictine monks in Germany, like all others on the Continent. They perhaps devoted themselves with more fervor to the work of transcribing the lives of the saints, and other pious books, than did their German brethren, and if some few of them quitted their own cloisters to enter a German monastery, they invariably settled down to a secluded and contemplative life.

In the thirteenth century a general and perceptible deterioration took place in all monastic life. Why should these foreigners whose institutions at this, the time of their highest prosperity, were already governed by the most rigid asceticism, and who were perfectly conscious of living as strangers in the land (and for this very reason of less importance as educators in Germany than the contemporary German monasteries), be expected to escape the universal degeneracy?   But there is an additional cause to account for the more rapid decline of the Irish monasteries than of the German ones of that part of the country.

Toward the end of the twelfth century (1171), began the subjugation of Ireland by the English.   It is a well-known fact that in 1154, Pope Hadrian IV. issued a bull presenting Ireland to the King of England, in consideration of the payment of a certain sum of tribute money, because the slight degree of independence assumed and maintained by the

Irish Church in regard to the Church of Rome was to the latter a thorn in the flesh, and not to be endured. The conquest of Ireland by the English, together with the existence of certain social evils, destroyed the real independence of its people, and, as a consequence, of the Irish Church.[1] The monks who now sought an abiding-place on the Continent—the aftergrowth of the old movement—no longer forsook their native land, as did Columbanus, to carry Christianity to the heathen;

[1] "It was a remarkable feature in the early evangelization of the Celtic race that it was originally far more independent of the influence of Rome than any of the German tribes were. In England the influence of the Irish and Scotch missions, though greatly thwarted by the pretensions of Rome, predominated in the north; while the authority of Rome was acknowledged in southern England. The Roman power gained the ascendancy only after a long struggle; but in Ireland especially, it was long before it was entirely established."

or, like Dungal, to instruct youth
eager for scientific knowledge; or
again, like Marianus and his col-
leagues, to exchange the transitory
for the eternal by means of a holy
life, far from home and kindred, but
to live in material comfort and
abundance, to be able to lead a life
of worldly freedom. *(Propter abun-
dantiam et propter liberam voluntatem
vivendi.)*

Intemperance is, even at the present day, Ireland's besetting sin.
Sedulius Scotus himself, when instructor at Liège, acknowledges his
love for the cup, in his invocations
to the Muses, and among his poetical
panegyrics is one addressed to a certain Robertus, who, rich in the possession of extensive vineyards, well
understood, according to Sedulius,
how to " awaken genius through the
inspiration of the heavenly dew."
Intemperance came to be, in fact,

the most prominent vice of the Irish monks of the numerous German monasteries. A satirical poem of the thirteenth century, by Nicolaus von Bibera, describes the orgies of some Irish monks of Erfurt, who boasted that Brendan was the brother of Christ, and St. Brigit his mother, drawing their logical conclusions thereto from the Holy Scriptures themselves, and in such a way as to show conclusively that they had indulged too freely in the " heavenly dew."

At the end of the thirteenth century, and later, these Irish monks, at a certain tavern in Nuremberg, held frequent and disgraceful orgies, drinking to such excess that they were often quite incapable of reading mass the next morning. In Vienna, they openly kept up their revels, pawned their chalices and vestments, as well as their chapel bells. Those who engaged in any occupation at all, took up trading in furs and other goods, so that the term " Irish monk " *(Scoti)* became synonymous with that of trader or pedlar.

The fate of their institutions was sealed. Some of them, like that of Oels, for example, came to an end through their own inherent weakness; others, like those of Vienna, Würzburg, and Eichstadt were made over to German monks, and in the Reformation lost, like that of Nuremberg, their monastic character. The mother monastery of St. James of Ratisbon underwent a most extraordinary transformation. During the fifteenth and sixteenth centuries, the truth was not understood, that, by the Irish or "Scots" were meant, from the earliest mediæval times, that nation alone which inhabited Ireland, and of which only a small portion had wandered to the north-western part of Britain, with which nation they became really incorporated, being now called Scotchmen, and their country being considered as thoroughly anglicized. The Scotch taking advantage of this, maintained on the ground of the designation *(monasterium Scotorum)* that the Scotch were the real founders of these institutions, and that the Irish had gradually and unlawfully intruded themselves into those monasteries,—hence their downfall. So in 1515, St. James was given to the Scotch by Leo. X., and all the Irish monks still living there were driven out.

This monastery, at the time of the Reformation, made a desperate effort in opposition to it, by assembling within its walls many able Scotchmen who were known to be inimical to the movement. But the characteristics of those later monks that lived here in the eighteenth century are often alluded to in the accounts of another Benedictine monastery of that time. In the year 1711, a Scotch Benedictine monk from the monastery of St. James of Ratisbon, by the name of Ambrosius Rosius, visited the monastery of Rheinau, and enjoyed its hospitality for a sojourn of several weeks. In this same monastery of Rheinau, where Findan had lived as an anchorite from 856 to 878, was preserved a copy of the *Vita* of Findan, before alluded to, with those celestial communications in the ancient Scotch, that is to say Irish, dialect. It is easily understood why the inmates of Rheinau should warmly welcome a guest who could unravel to them the meaning of those supernatural responses. These monks had as little understanding as any of that time, of

the very slight connection between
these *Scoti* of Ratisbon and those
monks and apostles of the seventh,
eighth, and ninth centuries mentioned in the manuscripts of that
time as *Scoti.* Ambrosius Rosius
probably spoke the language of
Ramsay and Burns, that is the
Scotch dialect of the English, which
corresponded about as fully with
that of Findan's voices from heaven,
as that of the *Isle de France* of the
early part of the eighteenth century
resembled the language in which the
" Gospel Harmonies " of Otfried
von Weissenburg[1] were written.
However, the Scotch brother from
Ratisbon showed his gratitude to the
monks of Rheinau for the generous
hospitality he had received by de-
ceiving them in the most shameless

[1] Otfried von Weissenburg, the Alsatian poet
and author, was educated at Fulda, and produced
his " Gospel Harmonies " in the year 868.

fashion.   He informed them that those ancient communications really signified: *ego debeo deo obtemperare et non tentationibus maligni spiritus.*

St. James of Ratisbon was secularized in 1860.

Although in the first century of the existence of this Scotch monastery, a few able men are to be found as inmates of it, the institution exercised no influence worth mentioning upon the general cultivation of the German people of that region, and may be considered as but a small contributor toward mediæval culture in general; for the only share that the Scotch monks can really claim in a monument like that of the church of St. James of Ratisbon, is the fact of their having collected the gold for its erection from the pockets of the Germans.

In comparison with these, how noble appear to us those apostles from Ireland, of whom we find so many traces in different parts of the kingdom of the Franks, from the beginning of the seventh to the end of the tenth century. We must go back to them for a few moments, in order to gauge them, or rather the culture which they represent, according to the acknowledged standards of our present civilization.

The two monasteries which we should consider as the true representatives of Irish culture on the Continent, even though the non-Irish element may be found to have been predominant in both, are Bobio, Columbanus' institution in Lombardy, and St. Gall, founded by his colleague Gallus in the country of the Alemanni. We are so fortunate as to be enabled to judge of the actual value of the libraries of both institutions at the close of the tenth century from old book-catalogues of both which have survived, and which were made in the ninth and tenth centuries. In Bobio the general library of the monastery at the end of the tenth, consisted of 700 volumes, comprising about 460 manuscripts of which the donor's name is not stated; and over 220 volumes presented to the monastery by different scholars of the ninth century, 40 of them being the gift of Dungal.

St. Gall possessed in the first half of the ninth century 428 volumes, to which 70 more were added under the Abbot Grimald, besides 35 presented by him (841–872); so at the end of the ninth century there were 533 volumes, 9 of them being palimpsests. When, in these days, large private libraries are incorporated into public ones, they are either catalogued and numbered differently from the rest, or a label or slip is pasted inside the covers of the odd volumes giving the name of the donor and former owner. Now, when it is known that the catalogue of Bobio enumerates 40 volumes given by Dungal, 32 by the presbyter Theodore, and 4 by Brother Adelbert, and that St. Gall possesses 35 manuscripts which the Abbot Grimald gave from his own private library, it follows that the most learned of the monks possessed, as a matter of course, their own private collections of choice works, which many of them bequeathed to the general library of the monastery.

With this wealth of manuscripts, the relative value of the contents of the two libraries may be considered about equal. Both these monasteries possess whatever was treasured and preserved of those writings, both religious and secular, of the most prominent scholars of the ninth and tenth centuries.   Beside theology taken in its broadest sense, the secular sciences were cultivated, as, for instance, grammar, metrics, astronomy, and medicine, as well as the best models of classical literature.   In the library at Bobio we find copies of Horace, Virgil, Ovid, Juvenal, Martial, Persius,[1] Terence, Cicero, Demosthenes, and Aristotle.

It is a well-known fact that when the holy fathers went to the Council of Constance taking no manuscripts with them, they had recourse to what the rich library of St. Gall could furnish them, and that when the council broke up (1418), very many of these pious men omitted or neglected to return those valuable old theological works in Latin and Greek.   Not less serious was the ad-

[1] Persius (Flaccus), was born in 34 and died in 62 A.D.   He was mostly distinguished as a satirist.

ditional loss sustained by the library
of St. Gall in another direction. In
the summer of 1416, Poggio, the
Florentine, and two scholarly friends,
who had been engaged with the
council, left Constance for St. Gall,
where, having a season of leisure,
they undertook a thorough search
for some missing volumes of Cicero,
Livy, and others. Their expecta-
tions were not disappointed, according to the letters they wrote to learned friends in Italy. Among others
there were the well-known "Argo-
nauticon" of Flaccus, copies of eight
of Cicero's orations with commentaries by Asconius Pedianus, [1] works of
the famous Roman architect Vitru-
vius, who lived in the reign of Au-
gustus, 30 B.C., of Priscian, Quinc-

[1] Asconius Pedianus, the learned grammarian
of Padua (30–60 A.D.), died during the reign of
Domitian. His commentaries on Cicero are of
much value.

tilian, Lucretius, and other great scholars. With the connivance of the abbot those precious manuscripts of classical literature were slipped into two wagons, carried to Constance, and from there into Italy, whence none of them were ever returned to St. Gall. And yet, in spite of all these losses, St. Gall still possesses a wealth of manuscripts, dating from the seventh to the eleventh century, in the way of works upon patristic theology, and of both classical and German antiquity.

It is no more true that the inmates of these two monasteries were, from the eighth to the twelfth century, exclusively Irish, or even that the Irish element greatly predominated in them, than that those invaluable manuscripts were all written by Irishmen, which they certainly were not. Still the works serve to represent the degree of culture attained by the Irish monks on the Continent during that period.

One circumstance must not be lost sight of in estimating the actual claim of the Irish monks as contributors to the literary treasures possessed by Bobio, St. Gall, Reichenau, and other monasteries. The Latin alphabet in use in Ireland in those times differs in many particulars from that in common use on the Continent, so that, as we have before observed, a Latin manuscript written by an Irish scholar, can be easily distinguished from one written by a continental hand. It is evident that those written by the Irish monks would present difficulties to the ordinary student on the Continent, and be an obstacle to a rapid comprehension of the same. This circumstance had important results. Those Irish monks who studied in the continental monasteries naturally tried, as far as possible, to accustom themselves to the forms of the letters most generally used on the Continent; of this we have the strongest evidence.

The whole mass of documents that we have seen, which were written by Moengal at St. Gall between 853 and 860, are undoubtedly originals and in the customary dialect and handwriting used in the middle portion of the ninth century, without the slightest traces of the so-called Scottish script; and those copies of the Epistles of St. Paul, (Codex 1247) to be seen at Vienna, which Marianus Scotus wrote in Ratisbon between the 23d of March and the 17th of May, 1079, are written, as I can state upon the authority of my own eyes, in the minuscule, the small handwriting peculiar to the Franks of that period, while his foot-notes and comments are written in the Irish way. Marianus used the Irish characters without doubt merely for his own private accommodation. This fact shows that very many of the manuscripts, ostensibly the work of continental scholars, may have been transcribed by Irish monks: and, regarding the manuscripts written in the genuine Irish manner, there is great probability of their having been brought with them from Ireland, there being no positive proof whatever of their having been of continental origin.

Moreover, those documents which were written in Ireland and carried to the Continent fell into disuse just as soon as they had been copied in any continental monastery. The fact seems to me in this connection not without significance, that in the old catalogue of St. Gall, drawn up in the ninth century, are enumerated 30 volumes in Irish script *(libri scottice scripti)*, and then is added, " A short list of the books belonging to the monastery of St. Gall *(breviarium librorum de cænobio sancti Galli confessoris Christi)* "; by this we assume that the former are undoubtedly verified as being those not in general use.

In after times, when not only every connection between the monasteries of St. Gall, Reichenau, and Bobio with Ireland was severed, but also because by reason of the general degeneracy of monastic life, real interest in and desire for the former peaceful life of the cloister had quite died out with the monks of these monasteries, the books written in Irish met with a still more disastrous fate. At St. Gall, at least, their value seems to have been estimated chiefly according to the condition of the parchment they were written upon; and in the fourteenth and fifteenth centuries the oldest manuscripts, including of course those written by the Irish, found their way into the workshops of the bookbinders. At St. Gall, early in the present century, six volumes of extracts were collected together, consisting of fragments and stray sheets from older manuscripts. Of the thirty volumes written by the Irish monks in the middle of the ninth century, only one remains, and but four of those of later date, while there are ten fragments or single leaves of manuscripts in the Irish character to be found at St. Gall.

In other places the books written by the Irish apparently met with a similar fate, for in this century such fragments have been occasionally met with in the various libraries on the Continent, and single stray leaves from volumes dating from the fourteenth and fifteenth centuries. *Libri scottice scripti,* both in the last and in the present century, have been brought to England, having been purchased or accidentally brought to light in some other way, as may possibly occur in rare instances.

It would be most interesting to know, after all these losses, what specimens may still be found on the Continent of those Irish manuscripts dating from the seventh to the eleventh century. The result of such a search would necessarily be somewhat unsatisfactory ; still, from what I have myself seen of the Irish manuscripts, extracts, and single leaves of that time, which are undoubtedly authentic, and from all that I can learn about them, I am led to the supposition that there must be at least two hundred of them in existence, and among these there are thirty-three which contain more or less important articles of varying length, written in the Irish language exclusively, which actually date from that period. The contents of the scanty remnants of earlier manuscripts possess also considerable value, not to mention the fact that Zeuss [1] gleaned from them the materials for his grammar of the ancient Irish language and laid the foundation of Celtic philology.

In the department of Biblical literature I will recall but two important examples: the Gospel Codex at St. Gall, written in Greek with a translation in Latin, and the *Codex Boernerianus*, now to be found in Dresden, which contains the Epistles of St. Paul in Greek, together with an interlinear Latin version of the same. Both of these works date from as early a period as the ninth century, and

[1] Johann Kaspar Zeuss, the famous historian and philologist, was born in 1806. In 1839 he became Professor of History at Spires, and in 1847 Professor of the Lyceum at Bamberg, where he produced his *chef-d'œuvre* " Grammatica Celtica " (1853), published at Leipsic. He died in 1856.

the last contains a passage in the ancient Irish dialect which expresses the harshest possible sentence upon Rome at that time :

A pilgrimage to Rome demands strenuous effort, with but meagre advantage. If thou findest not the Heavenly King thou seekest, in thine own country, or carry Him not with thee, thou wilt never find him there (Rome). It is all folly, madness, delusion, frenzy : to go on a pilgrimage to Rome is to court death and destruction, and to draw down upon thee the wrath of the Lord.

Among other Irish manuscripts of interest and value to the classical philologist there is now to be found in Berne one precious volume, written in Ireland at the end of the eighth or beginning of the ninth century, which contains commentaries and annotations on Virgil, Horace, and Ovid, beside rhetorical disquisitions and one of Bede's works. This volume was most probably carried to the Continent by Dungal, and was used in Pavia as a text-book. Of the grammarian Priscian we have seen three specimens—at St. Gall, Leyden, and Carlsruhe (earlier at Reichenau), and one fragment at Milan, from Bobio, as well as an authentic Irish recension of them. All these manuscripts, quite independent of each other, and yet of common origin, were produced in Ireland in the first half of the ninth century, and finally appeared on the Continent.[1]

In conclusion, we can form, in fact, from the preceding sketches, a com-

[1] At Basle there are three manuscripts in the town library, one of them being a beautiful Irish psalter, with a hymn in praise of Bridget and Patrick.

plete representation of Ireland's part in the development of general culture, from the seventh to the eleventh century.

The German tribes combining together had finally succeeded, after many vain onslaughts, in undermining the Roman Empire by mere brute force. The conquerors willingly accepted what ancient culture they found established in the lands they had become masters of, but not being capable of carrying it on, they dragged those vanquished Roman provinces down with them into the quagmires of barbarism into which, at the end of the sixth century, the whole West seems to have been hopelessly sunk.

Only on the " Emerald Isle " had ancient culture found a secure footing and an asylum ; here bloomed and flourished a Christianity which swayed the hearts and minds of the people,—a Christianity which was not consciously in opposition to that of Rome, but at the same time was quite independent of the Roman hierarchy and of Roman intolerance; and the supporters of this religion, the priestly leaders of the people, held firmly to the doctrines of the great fathers of the Church, Ambrosius and Augustine, with equal reverence for the ancient classics.

Such was the country which sent forth numerous apostles at the end of the sixth century and at the beginning of the seventh, to settle in the Merovingian kingdom of the Franks and among other German tribes, to establish missionary stations in which the noblest secular culture was fostered in conjunction with Christianity. The Carlovingian kingdom was fully converted from heathenism at the time that these Irish scholars came there and labored strenuously to spread among the various German and Roman peoples the most precious treasures of classical learning, in the spirit of an enlightened Christianity.

The opinion of the most able writer on the Carlovingian period, in regard to one representative of that time (Dummler's article on Alcuin in the "General German Biography"), may, with some modifications, be held, concerning all these men—viz.: that, among them all, not one was distinguished for remarkable originality, with the single exception of Johannes Scotus Erigena, and that the reputation of having opened up strictly new paths to knowledge cannot certainly be claimed for them. However, they were instructors in every known branch of science and learning of the time, possessors and bearers of a higher culture than was at that period to be found anywhere on the Continent, and can surely claim to have been the pioneers,—to have laid the corner-stone of Western culture on the Continent, the rich results of which Germany shares and enjoys to-day, in common with all other civilized nations.

INDEX.

A

Aedan, 20
Agilberct, 43
Agricola on the conquest of Ireland, 12
Alcuin, 44 ; on Irish monks, 30, 32
Aldhelm, 37, 41
Anagratum, or Annegray, 21, 26 *n.*
Anchorites, 88 *n.*
Anglo-Saxon art confounded with Irish, 16 *n.*
Anglo-Saxons frequent Irish monasteries, 36, 41
Animchad, 86
Arbogast the Younger, 7
Ausonius, 7
Aventinus, 98 *n.*

B

Bangor, monastery of, 21, 23 *n.*
Baptism, 34
Basilicas, 47 *n.*
Bavaria, Irish monks in, 31
Bobio, monastery of, 18 *n.*, 53 ; founded by
    Columbanus, 23, 28 *n.* ; its library, 114
Boniface or Winfrid, 35
Bregenz, 22

Made in the USA
Las Vegas, NV
23 March 2021

20026653R00085